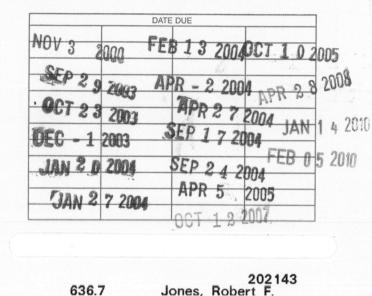

DATE DUE		
NOV 3 2000	FEB 1 3 2004	OCT 1 0 2005
SEP 2 9 2003	APR - 2 2004	APR 2 8 2008
OCT 2 3 2003	APR 2 7 2004	JAN 1 4 2010
DEC - 1 2003	SEP 1 7 2004	FEB 0 5 2010
JAN 2 0 2004	SEP 2 4 2004	
JAN 2 7 2004	APR 5 2005	
	OCT 1 3 2007	

636.7
Jon

202143
Jones, Robert F.

Jake : a Labrador
puppy at work and
play

LAUREL DELL SCHOOL
SAN RAFAEL SCHOOL DISTRICT

950884 01275   28185D   004

Robert F. Jones · Photographs by Bill Eppridge

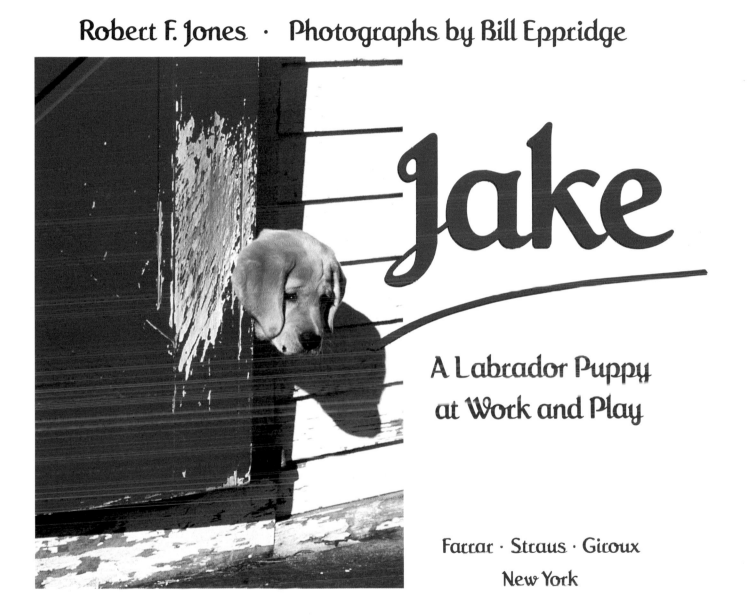

Jake

A Labrador Puppy
at Work and Play

Farrar · Straus · Giroux

New York

These words are for Grace Morris,
these pictures for Therese and Ep

Text copyright © 1992 by Robert F. Jones
Photographs copyright © 1992 by Bill Eppridge
All rights reserved
Published simultaneously in Canada by HarperCollins*Canada*Ltd
Color separations by Imago Publishing Inc.
Printed and bound in the United States of America by Berryville Graphics
First edition, 1992

Library of Congress Cataloging-in-Publication Data
Jones, Robert F.
Jake: a Labrador puppy at work and play / Robert F. Jones : photographs by
Bill Eppridge.—1st ed.   p.   cm.
Summary: The author describes his new Labrador puppy's first year and how he
trained the dog to sit, heel, fetch, and more.
   1. Labrador retriever—United States—Biography—Juvenile literature.   2. Labrador
retriever—Training—Juvenile literature.   3. Jones, Robert F.—Juvenile literature.
[1. Labrador retriever.   2. Dogs—Training.]   I. Eppridge, Bill, ill.   II. Title.
          SF429.L3J62   1992   636.7′52—dc20   92-8105   CIP   AC

Meet Jake, a yellow Labrador retriever. Looking at him just after he was born, you wouldn't think that in only a year he'd grow into a lovable, well-behaved member of our family, and a big, strong hunting dog.

Like their cousins the wolves, all dogs like to hunt—for food, mainly, but also for excitement, and for the sheer joy of the chase. Men and women who hunt with them can share that excitement, enjoy some wild-game dinners, and learn a lot about nature in the process.

Jake was born in August, but I had to wait until October, when he was eight weeks old, before I could bring him home. By this time his eyes were fully open. He could run and jump, although he was still very clumsy. He had stopped nursing and had learned to eat solid dog food. And the vet had made sure he'd had the full range of shots to prevent puppy diseases. Jake didn't mind the shots a bit. Puppies are tough.

Jake had two littermates, a brother named Hogan and a sister named Willa. Right from the start, though, Jake was the most outgoing. I suspected he was the dominant puppy in the litter. Jake seemed more sure of himself than the others, and I noticed that they followed his lead when they played.

Jake said goodbye to his first human friends, Grace and Myron Morris. They owned both of Jake's parents, and Grace had helped raise the puppies with lots of love and attention.

Jake's mother gave him a goodbye kiss, too. She didn't seem as unhappy as Grace did to see him go.

When we got home, Jake said hello to my black Labrador, Luke. Jake wanted to play, but the older dog was not about to get excited by a mere puppy. Luke was eleven years old, and since dogs age roughly seven times as fast as people, that would make him seventy-seven in human terms. He was willing to accept the puppy as a new member of the household so long as Jake didn't get all the attention. My wife, Louise, and I were careful to praise and hug Luke even more than usual to make sure he didn't feel neglected.

Next Jake met Spike, the family kitten. Spike was only about a month older than Jake, and because he'd already spent time around Luke, he was not afraid of dogs. And since Jake had never met a cat before, he was perfectly willing to play along.

Trouble was, they had different ways of playing. The first thing Jake tried to do was to retrieve Spike—by the head! Fortunately, Labradors have been bred to pick things up very gently when fetching them.

Spike's natural hunting weapons are his claws and teeth, and with animals, "play" is also a way to learn how to use one's weapons. So Spike responded by setting his claws lightly in Jake's fur and taking a firm grip on the puppy's ear with his sharp kitten teeth.

Jake was still teething, and his gums were tender where his new teeth were cutting through. Only by chewing on something could he relieve the itching. One day he found a tea cozy in the shape of a cat and carried it outside to gnaw on.

We quickly replaced it with something more suitable—a rawhide dog bone from the pet store—and out in the back yard, Jake found twigs and branches to chew.

All puppies want to have jobs to do in a family, and it's up to their human masters to train them for those jobs. Dogs who are not trained for a job, whether simple obedience or something more demanding, such as retrieving, sheepherding, Seeing-Eye work, or police duty, will invent jobs for themselves—and usually get into trouble. Dogs who dig up yards, dump garbage cans, chase cars, or pick fights with neighborhood cats and dogs are examples of family pets who have made up their own jobs.

The secrets of successful training are really quite simple. You must be patient, repeating the lessons over and over until they become second nature to the pup. You need to keep in mind that puppies have very short attention spans, and anything can distract them from a lesson—a butterfly fluttering past, a cat (like Spike) coming over to see what's going on, even another person standing by watching. Each lesson should be no more than twenty minutes long. And as soon as the pup seems to lose interest in the lesson, stop for a while and let him do something else. Whenever the pup does well, reward him with praise. Dogs are very sensitive to tones of voice, and you really can't praise them enough. The more you love your dog, the harder he'll work to please you.

Housebreaking came first. When Jake was inside, he slept in a small, portable puppy kennel, which we kept near us. Dogs will not soil their sleeping places, so as soon as Jake woke up from his many short naps, we would whisk him outdoors to do his business. He soon learned that "out" was the place to go—not on the kitchen or living room floor.

The second lesson I taught Jake was to sit. Holding one finger upright, I blew one short blast on a whistle and pressed his hindquarters down while saying, "Sit!" After a few lessons I didn't have to push his backside down anymore, and he would sit either at the vocal command, at the whistle blast, or when I raised my finger.

Next came "Stay!" With Jake sitting, I would keep my eyes fixed on his eyes and slowly back away from him, with my upraised hand facing him, palm open, and repeat, "Stay, Jake." When I was about twenty or thirty feet from him, I would blow two blasts on the whistle, say, "Come, Jake!" and make a sweeping come-here gesture with my arm. Again, he quickly learned to stay and come to any or all of the signals.

Then I taught him "Heel." With Jake on a light leash, I would position him at my side so that his nose was even with my foot. I said, "Heel, Jake!" and started walking. If he tried to pull ahead or cross in front of me, I would say "Whoa!" and pull him gently back to the heel position, then repeat the command and walk on. In a couple of weeks, I could walk him at heel without the leash.

At last Jake was ready for retrieving, his most important lesson —and by far the most fun. Labs are natural-born retrievers, but to make a formal game out of fetching not only brings out the best in the breed, it also teaches the puppy to be alert to his trainer's every wish or move. He learns to retrieve anything his master throws or points out or shoots at—a ball, a stick, a pair of bedroom slippers, a newspaper, a clay pigeon, or a game bird.

I started Jake out with a canvas-covered retrieving dummy called a bumper. I'd tell Jake, "Sit!" Then, "Stay!" While keeping firm eye contact with him, I'd throw the bumper out into the field behind our house. Only after it had landed would I say, "Fetch, Jake!" When he had picked it up, I would blow two blasts on the whistle and yell, "Come!"

Retrieving soon became his favorite game—more fun even than chasing and chewing on Spike.

Of course, I was training Jake to be a hunting dog, and needed to see how he would respond to the sound of gunfire. For this test, I had to have human help. A friend of mine named Sean Donovan and his eight-year-old son, Richard, provided it. Richard already knew that children must not handle guns—a

gun is a tool, not a toy—but he was glad of the chance to work with us.

While Richard held Jake at heel on a leash, Sean threw clay pigeons for me from my spring-loaded foot trap, and I shot the targets as they flew. Jake didn't flinch once, merely watched the clay birds fly and then shatter as I hit them. I had Richard bring Jake closer and closer as I shot. Soon Jake was sitting right at my feet, fascinated. When I finished, I unhooked Jake's leash. I made a throwing gesture in the direction of the clay pigeons and said, "Fetch, Jake!" He zoomed out as fast as his puppy legs could carry him, and trotted back, head held high, with the largest piece of clay pigeon he could find grasped gently in his mouth. He'd passed this test with flying colors.

But there were some things Luke could teach Jake better than I could. He quickly showed Jake how to climb over old stone walls as easily as climbing stairs. He proved to the pup that there was nothing to be afraid of if he poked his nose into a thorny patch of brush or a dark thicket of aspen saplings.

Luke knew where all the secret places in the woods were, especially the wet ones, and he led Jake down to the thickets around ponds and muddy brooks. Luke and Jake, being water dogs by birthright, loved to plunge into the ponds for a quick swim, or to cool off from the hot work of pounding up and downhill. They often rolled in the muddy streams or patches of marshland that lay in the swales.

By the time the hunting season ended just before New Year's Day, Jake had learned a lot. During the winter he played in the snow when I wasn't throwing the retrieving bumper for him. Luke, Jake, and I also took long afternoon walks through the snowy fields and woods. Jake learned not to chase after deer or rabbits when we came upon them. After all, Luke didn't chase them. Puppy see, puppy do—or don't, in this case.

When winter ended, Jake was twice his puppy size, maybe bigger. He no longer looked like a bear cub. His nose had lengthened, as had his legs and body and tail. He was turning into a handsome dog, as big as Luke though not as heavily muscled. He was calmer now, too, more mature. His attention span was longer, and the lessons I had taught him in his puppy days were second nature. But there was still a lot of the puppy in him, despite his size.

As spring came surging on, Jake exploded with all the extra energy he had stored up during winter. He ran through the fiddlehead ferns that sprouted almost overnight along the brook that runs behind our house.

He sniffed the flowers my wife had planted in the oak tubs near the back door, even tried to eat a few—until he decided that their taste wasn't up to their delicious smell.

Sometimes Jake picked the newly blossomed day lilies that grew around the edge of the house and pretended to be a trumpet player. At least, it seemed that way to me.

That summer, I wanted to see how Jake would feel about fishing. But he had other ideas . . .

Come fall, Jake was nearly full grown. He was a year old now, and as tall as he would ever get, but his chest would deepen and he'd put on more muscle over the next year or two. He weighed seventy-five pounds and would probably tip the scales at eighty-five when he reached his full size. Already he was bigger than Luke and outweighed him by a full five pounds.

Jake's friend Sweetz came for a visit, and the day suddenly turned into a galloping yellow whirlwind. The two young Labs looked so much alike that it was hard to tell them apart, especially when they were running—which they did, almost nonstop, all afternoon. Jake is the one on the left in both pictures.

But Jake hadn't forgotten his old friend and teacher, Luke. When Sweetz left, Jake sat at the back door and whined until Luke came out to join him. For an hour I threw the retrieving bumper for them. Then they just swam around together in our neighbor's trout pond, black Lab and yellow Lab, old dog and young dog, but brothers at heart. The sun was going down now, and as I sat beside the pond watching them, I thought about the year past. Luke and I had done a bang-up job. We'd taken a playful but scatterbrained puppy and helped him mature into a happy and well-mannered working dog. Luke, by his example, had taught Jake as much as I had—perhaps more.

They swam toward me, stroke for stroke, heads held proudly above the water. Both of them were grinning. I never loved them more.